Iceland Travel Guide

The Essential Guide To Iceland And
Top Things To Know Before Traveling

Russ Schinner

Copyright © Russ Schinner, 2022.

All rights reserved. No part of this publication may be reproduced, distributed, or transmitted in any form or by any means, including photocopying, recording, or other electronic or mechanical methods, without the prior written permission of the publisher, except in the case of brief quotations embodied in critical reviews and certain other noncommercial uses permitted by copyright law.

Table Of Content

Introduction

    Brief Iceland's History, Language, and Culture

    What You Should Know Before Your First Trip

    Best Time to visit Iceland

    Must try Food in Iceland

    23 Absolute-Best Places to Visit in Iceland (+Things to Do & Tips)

    Grand Golden Circle Day Trips in Iceland

    Some Secret Places Along Iceland's Golden Circle

    The Best Itineraries for Iceland from one day to two weeks

Introduction

Iceland is the ideal location for a seasoned tourist, a first-time solo traveler, or an adventurous family wishing to road drive throughout the island. With nice folks, gorgeous landscapes, loads of adventure, and a thriving tourist sector, you should visit Iceland at least once in your lifetime. I've come back twice already, and every journey delivers something fresh.

The highlights of my vacations have included a driving trip around Iceland's Ring Road, scuba diving the Silfra Fissure, visiting the Golden Circle, sampling local seafood in Reykjavik, and of course, lazing in the Blue Lagoon and various hot springs across the island. There is no lack of adventure in Iceland!

Iceland is full of magnificent sights and great experiences. The tranquility of the nation is considered the greatest in the whole globe. Visitors will discover perfect peace within the abundant natural heritage and also have interesting travels every day.

A Golden Circle Tour is great to discover the majesty and magnificence of Iceland on a single visit. It is regarded to be one of the greatest sites to explore in the nation. The whole circle comprises magnificent historical attractions, hot springs, lagoons, volcanic vistas, and geysers. Here we'll go over the techniques via which one may enjoy the greatest golden circle tour in Iceland.

Mother Nature has gifted Iceland with some of the most stunning landscapes, vivid skies, and unusual geological zones in the world. The country's stunning splendor and the outdoor activities built around this beauty are what initially draw most tourists to Iceland.

Without visiting one of Iceland's breathtaking waterfalls, no trip there is complete. The most famous waterfall in

Iceland, Gullfoss, is followed by Dettifoss, the most powerful waterfall in Europe, Skógafoss, a classic waterfall that is popular with tourists, Dynjandi, known for its distinctive trapezoidal shape, and so on. Visitors may spend a few busy, travel-filled days visiting each waterfall in turn. Iceland has at least 20 prominent waterfalls, so travelers with cameras who are trigger-happy may spend days taking pictures of these breathtaking locales.

Beyond waterfalls, Iceland also contains many other noteworthy outdoor attractions such as the famed Thingvellir National Park, the Great Geysir, the Blue Lagoon, the volcanic Mount Hekla, and the Kverkfjöll Ice Caves. As all these excellent locations are located around the nation, travelers may opt to schedule official trips with Icelandic Tours, Tourism, or Reykjavík Excursions. Those preferring to travel more freely may check into flights through the nation's most dependable domestic carrier, Air Iceland, or plan a bus trip via BSI (the country's statewide bus network), or hire a vehicle from a selection of major car rental firms present at the airports.

Travelers who prefer to make their journey a specifically-outside-bound one could consider contacting Arctic Adventures, an eco-adventure firm that specializes in outdoor adventure excursions that include rafting, glacier trekking, caving, ice climbing, kayaking, canoeing, and snorkeling.

Two, certainly, Iceland offers unlimited chances for outdoor sports; but let's not forget that it is also a nation that brought us Björk and some of the most varied electronica contemporary music listeners have heard in the previous decade or so. As one might expect, Reykjavk, the capital and largest city of the nation, has a robust music scene that includes a variety of genres from underground electronica to hardcore punk rock to indie to hip-hop to even classical chamber music.

Though Reykjavik, with its population of 170,000, may seem little in contrast to other international metropolises, it provides a more than pleasing attraction to tourists who may be weary of exploring nature. Its opera theatre, symphony, museums, and variety of cafés make it the nation's cultural center. The Reykjavik night scene is also thumping: guests may eat supper at the iconic landmarks The Pearl, or the Icelandic Bar; go partying at Pravda, Restaurant 22, or NASA; and even have some celebrity sightings at Kaffibarinn or Rex Bar.

Thinking of visiting Iceland and having any travel-related questions? This guide with our best advice for Iceland should give you a better sense of what to anticipate when going to Iceland for the first time, even if you have visited Iceland previously. These are experience-based Iceland travel advice that should address all your practical questions and help you prepare for your trip to Iceland. Find out!

Brief Iceland's History, Language, and Culture

A nation of tremendous geological differences, Iceland has built up an amazing tourist industry with over 2 million visitors a year coming to view its moss-covered lava fields, glacier-fed ice caverns, rock-ribbed beaches, and ash-spouting volcanos.

Widely known as "the country of fire and ice", Iceland is loaded with a breathtaking landscape that amazes and awes at every turn. The term fire in the phrase relates to Iceland's many volcanoes, which spring into life occasionally. Elemental forces boil just below the surface around the nation, and savvy Icelanders have long been using geothermal energy to create power, heat tap water, and warm up tomato gardens.

Volcanic tourism is also profitable, with visitors taking treks to witness bursting fumaroles and bask in thermal springs. The two notable examples of the latter are the Blue Lagoon and Sky Lagoon in Reykjavík; both are geothermal spas that try to heal your aches and pains.

Ice is Iceland's second huge lure (the hint is in the name) - more especially, the majestic glaciers that carve down towards the shore, calving icebergs into tranquil lagoons. About 11% of the nation is covered in glaciers, with Vatnajökull being the biggest and reaching some 8,400km² (3,243mi) in the southeast with thick layers of snow blanketing numerous high, spectacular mountain slopes. Iceland's tallest mountain, Hvannadalshnjúkur (2,119m or 6,592ft) may also be located here. Guided trips to glaciers, ice caves, and frozen waterfalls are frequently offered.

Reykjavík, Iceland's capital city, is where most tourists start their adventure. This exciting and colorful city, with its numerous museums, marine excursions, and vivid nightlife, is surely a great detour.

So come to experience wandering in a lava cave, climbing a glacier, sighting a whale, or watching the beautiful northern lights In their full grandeur, undimmed by light pollution in the least densely inhabited country in Europe. No matter what you do, a trip to Iceland is an experience you'll remember for a lifetime.

Iceland History, Language, and Culture

History of Iceland

Iceland was colonized by Norse seamen more than 1,000 years ago and they first convened in Þingvellir (now Thingvellir National Park) in the year 930.

In 1262, Iceland surrendered to the King of Norway, and Jónsbók (the code of laws) was presented to the islanders in 1281. In 1397, the establishment of the Kalmar Union saw Denmark, Sweden, and Norway, together with Norway's possessions such as Iceland and Greenland, all fall under the sovereignty of Denmark. In 1814, Norway became independent, but Iceland remained a Danish province. In 1944, Iceland earned its independence and the new nation has been commemorating its National Day on 17 June ever since.

Did you know?

Iceland outlawed all alcoholic beverages in 1915. Then over the decades, it eventually authorized red wine and spirits, but beer remained outlawed until 1 March 1989 - the day is today commemorated as Bjordagur (Beer Day).

Many Icelanders believe in the presence of huldufólk (hidden people or elves), who have been part of the Icelandic tradition for generations.

Icelanders do not use family names but take the first name of their father or mother as a last name, adding the suffix son (meaning son) or dóttir (meaning daughter) (meaning daughter).

Iceland Culture

Religion in Iceland

About 80% of Icelanders are Lutherans and another 5% belong to other Christian groups. About 5% of the inhabitants still practice ásatrú, the old Norse religion.

Social Conventions in Iceland

Iceland boasts a 99% literacy rate - its inhabitants are informed, well-spoken, and quite courteous. Icelandic is the native language although Danish and English are frequently spoken.

Icelanders love enjoying a warm dip in a sundlaug (heated pool) or a geothermal spa, with many visiting a pool regularly. In any public pool, the following bathing etiquette must be observed:

Remove your shoes before entering the locker room. Upon entering, use the bracelet you've got at the reception to access a locker. Put away your phone since no photography is permitted (unless you are attending a tourist-oriented geothermal spa like the Sky Lagoon).

Undress and put away your clothing, but take your swimsuit and towel to the shower room and place them in one of the storage units there. Wash completely without your swimwear. If you feel uncomfortable, utilize one of the private stalls.

Head to the pool while wearing your swimsuit. After that, relax in the hot tub.

Once you're done, continue to the shower area and wash again. You must then dry off (with the towel you left in the shower room earlier) before entering the locker room.

Put on your clothes and visit the hair-drying section if you desire.

Leave the locker room and put on your shoes outdoors.

Drop your wristband into a box, which will unlock the turnstile so you may exit.

Language in Iceland

The official language is Icelandic; English and Danish are frequently spoken.

Phrases
Beer (Bjór)

Closed (Lokað)
Danger (Haetta)
Doctor (Læknir)
Entrance Inngangur (noun)
Exit (Útgangur)
Goodbye (Bless)
No (Nei)
Open (Opid) (Opid)
Restaurant (veitingastaður)
Thank you (Takk or Þakka þér)
Hello (Hæ or Halló)
Hotel (Hótel)
How are you? (Hvernig hefurdu thad?)
Menu (Matseðill)
My name is (Ég heiti)
Today (Í dag)
Toilets (Klósett or salerni)
Tomorrow (Á morgun)
Where is...? (Hvar er ...?)
Wine (Vín)
Yes (Já)

What To Expect

Language: The predominant language spoken is Icelandic, as well as English in the tourist parts.

Currency: The currency of Iceland is the Icelandic króna, however, many shops will also take the Euro and the US Dollar. 1 USD is comparable to roughly 119,60 ISK.

NOTE: Iceland can be VERY pricey, so be sure to check out my Tips for Traveling Iceland on a Budget!

What You Should Know Before Your First Trip

We have gone to Iceland numerous times. We've gone to Iceland in winter and in summer. I went alone, as a couple, and with kids. We drove in a standard vehicle and with a 4WD, driving the Ring Road and exploring the highlands, but also with a group excursion in winter...

So our Iceland travel advice is based on our own experience in Iceland throughout all those travels. It's not a guide based on a single trip like most others that you'll find... This collection of Iceland travel tips comprises all the most significant things that we believe are vital or interesting to know before visiting Iceland.

Furthermore, we operate Iceland and Scandinavia travel groups on Facebook where we see many identical queries come up again and again. Do I need to carry cash to Iceland? Do I require a 4WD or can I travel the Ring Road with a standard car? What sort of footwear do I need for Iceland? Is a travel adapter or a converter required for Iceland? What type of weather might I expect? Can I drive the complete Ring Road in 5 days in winter? And how come I don't discover any reasonable accommodations for my vacation next week? ....

So in this post, we compiled all the Iceland FAQs in one spot. I hope that this advice will help you better prepare for your trip to Iceland and get the most out of it. Find out!

1. Book in advance

This is one of the most vital travel recommendations for Iceland. You need to schedule everything for your Iceland vacation far in advance!

From flights to rental vehicles and from lodging to excursions – make sure that you arrange everything well beforehand. The more you wait, the less option you have and the more you'll pay.

The best price/quality hotels are the first ones to be completely booked, and the greatest prices for car rental cannot be obtained upon arrival at the airport (in fact, there may not be any vehicles available at all - this happens all the time), and the finest excursions sell out too. And yes, even the famed Blue Lagoon needs to be reserved in advance.

So if you want to make your Iceland vacation more reasonable and stress-free, do yourself a favor and book as much as you can beforehand.

2. Don't use cash

One of the most commonly asked questions I see again and again is 'do you need cash in Iceland?'. It's as if people read about it and yet cannot believe that you don't. So, once again, currency is not required in Iceland.

Nordic nations are famed for their nearly nonexistent cash payments and Iceland is no exception.

Paying using credit or debit cards is feasible anywhere in Iceland. EVERYWHERE. Even a 200ISK (1.5EUR) charge for the use of a restroom at Thingvellir National Park may be paid by credit card. This is perhaps a horrible example since now you assume that using a restroom is pricey in Iceland. Thingvellir is really one of the rare sites where you have to pay for the restroom.

Agreed, holding foreign money in your hands could make your vacation experience seem more real. But if money is only a method of payment to you, spare yourself all the bother and useless spending towards the conclusion of the vacation in order to get rid of the cash, and use your credit card instead.

Good to know: Iceland utilizes Icelandic króna and no, you cannot pay with euro or in the US currency. If you really want to carry cash, take an equivalent of about 50-80 USD. That should be more than enough for modest expenses where credit cards aren't accepted. As I write this, I truly can't think of one single situation when we couldn't use a credit card in Iceland. But several individuals in our FB group stated that 'certain bathrooms only accept cash.

3. Use credit cards with a pin

You may use all major credit cards in Iceland, although VISA and Mastercard are by far the best. Amex is not often recognized and Diner's Club is pretty much worthless. Debit cards (or cash-only cards) are also routinely accepted.

One thing you should know is that you should carry a card with a chip and a 4-digit

PIN to Iceland. Make sure you remember your PIN number! You'll need a credit card for all the payments all around Iceland – from restaurant bills to gas stations – and the quickest method to pay is by utilizing the card with a pin.

Good to know: Many of our American readers indicate that they were able to use their standard credit cards with simply a swipe and a signature all around Iceland except at unmanned gas stations. So if you don't have a credit card with a pin and prefer not to obtain one, you might get a prepaid gasoline card upon arriving in Iceland. That way you may use that card at unmanned gas stations that have no stores or workers.

The only difficulty with these prepaid cards is that you have to attempt to predict how much money to put into them from the start and it's not always straightforward. Furthermore, you'll only be able to use this arrange everything well beforehand. The more you wait, the less option you have and the more you'll pay.

The best price/quality hotels are the first ones to be completely booked, and the greatest prices for car rental cannot be obtained upon arrival at the airport (in fact, there may not be any vehicles available at all - this happens all the time), and the finest excursions sell out too. And yes, even the famed Blue Lagoon needs to be reserved in advance.

So if you want to make your Iceland vacation more reasonable and stress-free, do yourself a favor and book as much as you can beforehand.

2. Don't use cash

One of the most commonly asked questions I see again and again is 'do you need cash in Iceland?'. It's as if people read about it and yet cannot believe that you don't. So, once again, currency is not required in Iceland.

Nordic nations are famed for their nearly nonexistent cash payments and Iceland is no exception.

Paying using credit or debit cards is feasible anywhere in Iceland. EVERYWHERE. Even a 200ISK (1.5EUR) charge for the use of a restroom at Thingvellir National Park may be paid by credit card. This is perhaps a horrible example since now you assume that using a restroom is pricey in Iceland. Thingvellir is really one of the rare sites where you have to pay for the restroom.

Agreed, holding foreign money in your hands could make your vacation experience seem more real. But if money is only a method of payment to you, spare yourself all the bother and useless spending towards the conclusion of the vacation in order to get rid of the cash, and use your credit card instead.

prepaid card at the same chain, so make careful to select a major one like N1.

TIP: If you don't have a suitable credit card and want to acquire a new one, check out our pick of the top American credit cards for travel. I suggest using a card with no international transaction fees (and a pin!).

4. Be prepared for the ever-changing weather

It always makes me grin when folks question what type of weather they'll receive in a given trip time. It's simply difficult to respond. Yes, it will be colder in January than in July, but that's as much an accurate prognosis as anybody can give you...

Icelandic weather is so unpredictable that it may shift from winter to summer in only a day. Gulf Stream keeps Iceland cool in summer and gentle in winter. The average temperature in Reykjavik is approximately

0°C (31°F) in January and just 13°C (55°F) in July.

No matter when you visit Iceland - in summer, in winter, or any time in between, you ALWAYS have to be prepared for all sorts of weather. It may (and it will) change numerous times a day. You may start the day in magnificent sunlight, get soaking soaked in a torrential rainstorm or blown by the incredible wind an hour later, and finish up driving in a mist with zero visibility another couple of hours later... You simply never know.

Also, don't rely on weather prediction alone. Often, the temps could appear good, but the wind makes a tremendous difference.

5. Wear many layers of clothing and a waterproof outer layer.

You will need casual clothing in layers for trips and some sophisticated outfits for heading out. Warm wind- and a waterproof jacket and a swimsuit are important all year round.

In summer or in winter, always dress in layers and always have a waterproof outer layer at hand, A decent waterproof jacket is necessary. So are excellent waterproof boots and waterproof rain trousers. You should also always carry a buff, a pair of gloves, and a thick cap with you.

Below you may discover our advice for what to bring to Iceland in every season. The summer list is for mid-May to mid-September and the winter list applies for the balance of the year (October to April-May). Bookmark these articles or download our packing lists to make sure you're not missing anything vital.

6. Pack waterproof shoes

If you want to enjoy your Iceland vacation to the utmost, strong sturdy shoes are a requirement. In summer, I suggest decent waterproof hiking boots, and in winter — warm solid winter boots with a good grip.

I wore these Lowa hiking boots in Iceland in summer and these UGG waterproof winter boots in Iceland in winter.

Once, I brought water-resistant hiking boots to Iceland but realized that it actually wasn't enough. Waterproof shoes are truly a requirement in Iceland in any season!

You certainly need nice waterproof shoes in order to enjoy your Icelandic vacation to the utmost!

7. Keep an eye on weather advisories and road closures

Make careful to constantly check whether there are any weather advisories or road closures while driving in Iceland. While it's always a good idea to keep an eye on the weather forecast and any safety warnings, it's very vital to do this if visiting Iceland outside of the summer season.

In winter, several roads in Iceland are blocked. And even portions of the key roadways like the Ring Road can be blocked due to snowfall or similar. It's crucial that you examine whether there are any

You may anticipate all types of weather in Iceland, but it's always magnificent, even on the dismal days

8. Know how much to spend on your vacation

Iceland is not a cheap nation, however, most expenditures may be compared to how much things cost in other Scandinavian countries or Switzerland. The most costly items are hotels, eating out, and planned activities.

TIP: You may save a lot of money by reserving items in advance.

9. You don't have to tip

It's not common to tip in Iceland and tips are not expected. Your restaurant bill is big enough as it is and service is already included in it.

Many people prefer to tip tour guides in Iceland. However, although always appreciated, it's also not necessary. If you want to tip your tour guides, you may wish to take some cash. Many folks merely tip in USD or EUR.

How costly is Iceland - pricing samples for meals, accommodation, car hire, activities, and more

Icelandic sweaters — one of the most costly, but also handy souvenirs you can purchase in Iceland

10. Drive cautiously

Iceland has right-hand traffic. Driving in Iceland is incredibly peaceful since there is seldom any traffic outside of Reykjavik. In summer, it's simple to tour Iceland via the major Ring Road by automobile.

However, most key highways in Iceland, including the greatest stretches of the Ring Road, have only one lane in each direction and no shoulder. It's thus incredibly crucial that you drive cautiously and maintain your eyes on the road all the time. You have to expect sheep and visitors on the road - the latter frequently even more irresponsible and unpredictable.

Do not stop on the side of the road, since others won't be able to simply pass you.

It's also useful to know that Iceland has several single-lane bridges and even some single-lane tunnels. There are usually indications stating who has precedence and how to approach it, but you have to drive slowly enough to read those signals in time!

Driving in the cold is an entirely different affair. Expect ice roads, snow on the highways, the wind that blows so much snow that you can't see anything, and darkness. Even if you have winter driving expertise at home, driving in Iceland in the winter is an entirely different ballgame. Please do not drive if you have no winter driving expertise. You will be doing yourself and others a favor. There are numerous organized tours available. It is not worth your life!

11. Know when you need to hire a 4WD or 4×4

No, you don't need a 4WD or a 4×4 in Iceland. The Ring Route is paved and most sights along this famous road may easily be visited in a typical 2WD vehicle.

That being said, if you are heading to Iceland in winter (October to April/May), a 4WD or a 4×4 is always a smart choice.

Also in summer, if you are going to venture a little off the beaten route and visit some sites like the lighthouses of Snaefellsnes Peninsula, the cliffs of Reykjanes Peninsula, or the Westfjords, to name just a few, you may also consider hiring a 4WD. You need an automobile that is permitted to drive on the F-roads. It really makes your journey so much less stressful and more pleasurable!

12. Know what the F-roads are

You may have heard of the F-roads in Iceland, but what are they? The F-roads are minor roads in Iceland and generally, they are gravel. However, one F-road is not equivalent to another. While some F-roads are only basic gravel roads, while others are exceedingly rough, and some include severe river crossings.

Driving the F-roads needs a 4WD or a 4×4. In certain circumstances, it takes a 4x4super jeep.

Most F-roads are normally only available from mid-June to approx. end September (weather depending) (weather dependent). If you are intending to drive any F-roads, make sure that you conduct appropriate research and know which roads are good with a conventional 4WD or a modest 4×4 and which ones demand a 4×4 super jeep.

Make sure that you hire a vehicle that is suited for the roads you are going to drive and that your rental agreement enables you to operate that car on the F-roads. Please take know that even the greatest and the most extensive insurance does not cover river crossings.

13. Take comprehensive insurance for your automobile

I can't even tell you how frequently I read this question - 'Do I really need 100% insurance coverage for my rental vehicle in Iceland?'. The answer is yes!

While it is extremely probable that nothing will happen and you won't need your auto insurance, the odds are fairly high that you will need it. And in such a scenario, the repair expenses would be huge…

I've read tens of accounts from individuals whose vehicle glass was broken by flying pebbles or whose car doors were ripped-off by high winds in Iceland, and those who didn't buy comprehensive insurance, end up spending a lot of money for these mishaps that they couldn't even do anything about…

Our experience: We've traveled to Iceland multiple times and thankfully we had full insurance every time. On our first journey (end of May-beginning of June), we faced snowfall and slippery roads and our vehicle skidded off the road. Luckily, there was no damage to the vehicle or the passengers, but at least we didn't have to worry about the insurance, only getting our car back on the road…

On our most recent journey, we experienced a flat tire in the Westfjords. It was severely destroyed beyond repair and our insurance reimbursed the replacement tire that we purchased. We didn't even have to prepay for it — the automobile rental company phoned the garage and straightened it all out.

TIP: I suggest hiring your automobile using the RentalCars website. Not only can you compare numerous providers and get the best discounts for your rental vehicle, but you are also much more protected in case a local firm goes bankrupt as it recently did with our favorite local supplier in Iceland. Our experience with Rental Cars has always been fantastic.

14. Make a road trip

Now that I informed you that driving in Iceland isn't always simple or recommended, I also want to stress that hiring a vehicle and road-tripping is also the finest way to experience Iceland.

Public transit choices are quite restricted and day trips are rather pricey. In winter, I suggest taking tours from Reykjavik or a multi-day scheduled vacation like this, but in summer you may easily explore Iceland on your own.

Staying in Reykjavik and seeing all the greatest sites by taking tours isn't optimal (except in winter) and I definitely suggest enjoying Iceland by taking a road trip. The most popular spots along the South Coast of Iceland may be visited in as little as 4-5 days. Here you may discover a highly thorough itinerary encompassing all the must-see locations in the south of Iceland: 4 days in Iceland.

If you wish to visit the full Ring Road, I suggest at least 10-12 days. See our suggested 10-day Iceland Ring Road itinerary on how to best manage your time.

With a week in Iceland, you can visit all the very finest spots in the south and the west. Here you may find our suggested one-week Iceland itinerary.

15. Research where to go and what to see

Iceland is so huge and there is so much to see that it's incredibly hard to see all the greatest spots in only a few days. A lot also depends on the time of year you travel. It's, thus, vital to perform some research in preparation.

The most popular destinations to visit are Reykjavik, the Golden Circle, the Blue Lagoon, the waterfalls and the black sand beaches of the South Coast, and also the Jokulsarlon Glacier Lagoon. Our 4-day itinerary stated above includes all these must-see attractions.

If you have the time, though, I definitely urge that you explore Iceland further. Because it has so much more to offer than that!

16. Get off the beaten path

Iceland has become such a popular trip and certain spots are incredibly crowded. Reykjavik, the Blue Lagoon, and the major sites along the south coast may become highly busy at any time of the year... And also the Myvatn region in summer...

The good news is that there are still lots of great spots in Iceland that are not yet overrun by visitors and where you can enjoy the most magnificent environment and local life without the masses.

Icelandic highlands are, of course, like that, but most spots there aren't readily accessible. However, there are many conveniently accessible spots that are not crowded at all. Here are just a few examples of some wonderful less-visited spots in Iceland that we simply love:

Raudasandur Beach
Dynjandi Waterfall
Haifoss Waterfall
Reykjanes Peninsula
Westman Islands
Siglufjordur
Trollaskagi Peninsula

Hvitserkur

17. Get a Wi-Fi hotspot or mobile data bundle

There is decent mobile network coverage pretty much everywhere in Iceland. Even on my vacation exploring the Icelandic Highlands, we had 4G cell network service practically everywhere. I was having video conversations with my kids from some of the most magnificent spots in the middle of nowhere.

All hotels and most eateries in Iceland feature free high-speed Wi-Fi.

If you have a SIM card from any of the EU nations, you won't be charged any roaming costs in Iceland.

If you are coming from the US, I propose that you either rent a portable Wi-Fi device. They are available for hire at the airport and certain automobile rental firms provide them as well. You may connect many gadgets to it and enjoy decent internet throughout your whole journey.

Some individuals opt to additionally acquire a local SIM card, although I don't understand why you'd need one if you had a portable wifi device or a mobile data pack. You may make phone calls using WhatsApp or other applications on your phone.

18. Learn a few words of Icelandic

If you speak English, you have nothing to worry about while visiting Iceland. Everyone appears to speak English therefore you will not need to learn Icelandic. However, it could be beneficial to learn a few words of Icelandic. Even if merely to better grasp the names of the sites you'll be seeing.

Remember the difficult name of the volcano that erupted a few years ago —

Eyjafjallajökull? Ask Icelanders how to say it so you can wow everyone back home.

Just a comment about Icelandic place names. The lengthy hard words are only a compilation of lesser ones.

So, for example, the above-mentioned Eyjafjallajökull means 'the glacier of an island mountain': eyja (island), fjalla (mountain), and jökull (glacier) (glacier). Reykjavik (bay of smokes): reykja (smoke) and vik (bay), etc.

Here are some additional prominent terms that you'll find utilized in the place names throughout Iceland: foss = waterfall, vik=bay, fjordur= fjord, dalur= valley, Vegur=road, gata=street, gljúfur=canyon, jökull=glacier, fjall=mountain, and fjöll=mountains...

19. Drink tap water

Tap water in Iceland is safe and it's pretty excellent. Make sure to carry a reusable drinking container for your day outings and fill it with tap water.

There is virtually no incentive to purchase bottled water in Iceland. All restaurants give tap water for free - here is a healthy approach to saving money.

20. Enjoy the finest of Iceland for free

The finest things in life are free, and so are the best things in Iceland. There are no admission fees to any of the most renowned sites. Waterfalls, glaciers, geysers, national parks - you may see them all for free.

21. Don't overlook the nearby hot springs and pools.

While everyone constantly speaks about the renowned geothermal pools such as the Blue Lagoon, Sky Lagoon, Myvatn Nature Baths, and a few more, most people forget that Iceland is a nation of swimming pools. Every town and most smaller communities in Iceland have a pool. And not just any pool!

Most local pools in Iceland are first-class facilities. Often, these are outdoor pools that also contain many hot tubs, saunas, and steam baths. Many local pools also feature baby pools, water toys for youngsters, or even water slides. Furthermore, these pools cost only a fraction of the popular ones, and there are rarely any people there.

There are also several natural hot springs all across Iceland where you are permitted to swim.

So while planning your vacation, be sure to look for nearby pools or hot springs. It's the ideal way to conclude your day of touring! Every day!

22. Pack European travel adapters

In Iceland, the power is 220 volts and you have to use European type C adapters.

For typical gadgets such as mobile phones, a basic travel adaptor is sufficient. For hefty gadgets, you'd need a converter, however, I'd recommend leaving such items at home. Most hotels include hair dryers.

23. Prepare for limitless days in summer and only a few hours of daylight in winter

Here are just a few samples of what to anticipate in terms of daylight while visiting Iceland:

In summer, the sun never sets in Iceland, thus the days are limitless. If you come in May or June, you have pretty much 24 hours of daylight.

If you visit Iceland at the beginning of April or the beginning of September, you will enjoy roughly 14 hours of daylight.

In December, you'll get about 3-4 hours of daylight in Southern Iceland and just 2-3 hours of daylight in North Iceland. It's crucial to plan your winter vacation to Iceland wisely, otherwise, you won't see anything.

Good to know: Iceland is in the GMT zone, therefore there is a 1-hour difference from the UK and 2 hours from Western Europe. Iceland's local time is four hours earlier than New York's.

24. Know what to anticipate while hunting for the Northern Lights

Many tourists visit Iceland expecting to experience the Northern Lights. And the fact, Iceland is a terrific destination for it! You may expect to observe auroras between

September and March - mid-April, but it remains a chance.

There are several things that you should know and also some strategies that will boost your chances to observe the Northern Lights. We developed a thorough guide addressing all the questions and offering all our best suggestions for aurora hunting in Iceland.

25. Pack sleeping masks in summer

If you want to enjoy your summer vacation in Iceland, you certainly need to carry a sleeping mask. Most hotels and lodgings do not have complete black-out curtains and because it remains bright the whole night, you won't get any sleep without covering your eyes.

26. Pack crampons in winter

Most locals and visitors who have experienced a genuine winter wonderland in Iceland suggest carrying crampons or stabilisers when visiting Iceland in winter. The pavements in town may be ice and walking trails around the waterfalls can seem like an ice skating rink. If you want to securely enjoy your winter excursion, it's extremely essential to put ice cleats over your shoes.

27. Stay safe

Iceland is a highly safe nation and the crime rate is quite low. To give you an idea, the entire jail capacity in Iceland is roughly 120 convicts, and it's more than adequate. If there is one nation in the world where you don't have to worry about safety, then it has to be Iceland.

That being said, lately, there have been quite a few incidences of individuals being robbed by pickpockets at the prominent natural sights around the Golden Circle. So it never damages to be extra diligent.

The largest threat for visitors is driving, unexpected weather, and uncontrolled conduct in nature. So keep a watch for warnings, follow the signs at the cliffs, waterfalls, and beaches and be sure to drive properly.

And if you are visiting an active volcano, don't step on lava! It could appear like it's hard already, but frequently, there's still a lot of activity below and the crust is extremely thin!
Iceland active volcano - Fagradalsfjall eruption
Fagradalsfjall volcanic eruption in Iceland. Many visitors visiting the volcano have been observed strolling on a thin layer of lava - don't do that, it's highly hazardous!

So, these are some of our important travel advice for Iceland.

Best Time to visit Iceland

Wondering when is the ideal time to travel to Iceland and what to anticipate in every season? This guide should give you a better understanding of what it's like to visit Iceland in various seasons and to select when to come to Iceland. Find out!

Iceland is one of those destinations that you can visit all year round. It's harsh and beautiful at the same time, it's distinctive, and it will undoubtedly surprise you. First-time tourists frequently play it safe and come to Iceland in the summer. However, lately, more and more tourists discover this magnificent nation in winter. But when to visit Iceland?

The ideal time to visit Iceland depends on what you anticipate from your vacation. Below in this essay, we explore the key pros and cons of visiting Iceland in summer versus winter.

If you are afraid about the weather in Iceland, all I can say is don't worry, since there is just nothing you can do about it. Of course, statistically speaking, you will get warmer and drier weather in summer than in winter, but it doesn't guarantee that it will be that way. It wasn't when we traveled...

My own experience in Iceland in summer, autumn, and winter

I visited Iceland numerous times: in May – June, in July, in August, in September, and in November. Below, you may read about my experience on each of these trips.

Further down, you may see a comparison of experiences and activities that you can do in Iceland in summer vs winter. Based on what you wish to see and do, should enable you to decide when to visit Iceland. Read on!

Iceland in May – June

The day we arrived in Akureyri on the 31st of May 2006, we found ourselves in the thick of a tremendous snowfall. Our aircraft had trouble landing, the roads were slippery and several portions of the major route around the island were blocked, the streets were blanketed with snow, and nearly everything was closed.

The rental vehicle firm upgraded us to an SUV since they didn't believe it was safe to travel with a standard car. Despite this, our automobile found itself in a ditch on the second day of the trip...

Luckily, nobody was wounded and there was no damage to the automobile. We were very fortunate that a kind Icelander happened to be passing by within only a few minutes on an empty road, and that he had all the tools to get our vehicle back on the road with his monster-size 4×4.

Just two days later all the snow was gone and we even had one bright day with temperatures reaching 20°C (68°F) for just a brief minute. By the conclusion of our trip, we were wearing our winter coats again.
Snow in northern Iceland in June
Northern Iceland in June 2006

Iceland in November

So when I scheduled my winter vacation to Iceland in November many years later, I was prepared for anything.

It was chilly, much colder than imagined, but it was dry! There was some ice on the roads near Reykjavik on the first day, but we haven't seen snow or rain for the remainder of the week.

We were informed that it was exceedingly uncommon to have 7 dry days in a row in November. Just as it was exceedingly rare to see knee-high snow in June...

Beautiful winter scenery at Skaftafell National Park in Iceland
Beautiful winter scenery of Skaftafell National Park - November

Iceland in September

My third time in Iceland was in September, for an outstanding Icelandic highlands excursion. We had great sunny days, but also some rain and wind. One minute we would be strolling around in sweaters and an hour later we would need a winter jacket... But in general, it was bright - the nicest weather you could expect in Iceland.

We were informed by the locals that they didn't get as much sun over the full summer this year as we did in September...
Walking in a moss field in Iceland's highlands in September\sSeptember weather is typically as nice as in July in Iceland

Iceland in July

Recently I also got an opportunity to swiftly visit Iceland in July. It was merely a brief layover while going to and also back from Greenland. This happened in the summer of 2019, which was undoubtedly one of the prettiest, sunniest, and hottest summers Iceland had experienced.

The weather was wonderful in Iceland in July and we were roaming around Reykjavik in t-shirts. I also observed several individuals wearing shorts and sandals — an exceedingly unusual sight in Iceland.

Our Icelandic friends welcomed us for supper at their home where a number of their friends had gathered for a garden party. This was in the middle of the week and most folks arrived straight from work. They advised us that the weather is so spectacular that you had to take advantage of it while it lasts. 'Use the weather' they instructed us. Who cares that you have to go back to work the following morning...

That being said, even this extremely bright and mild Icelandic summer meant that maximum temperatures were about 15-18°C (59-64 F), with only a few days of temperatures exceeding 20°C (68 F) (68 F).

Iceland in August

Our most recent journey to Iceland comes in the second part of August. This was the same abnormally dry and warm summer of 2019. This trip, we spent ten days exploring West and North Iceland.

On the Snaefellsnes Peninsula, where our trip began, the weather was breathtakingly wonderful. We also experienced spectacularly sunny days in the North Icelandic Westfjords, Hvitserkur, and Siglufjordur. The sun had set by the time we arrived at the Myvatn region, but the weather was still dry and comfortable enough to wear only a sweater.

The weather did, however, change a week later, and by the time we traveled to the highlands, it was freezing, with some of the worst wind and horizontal rain. One day, we found it difficult to exit the car, so we had to switch our destination from Landmannalaugar to Haifoss.

At the end of the tour, when we returned to the Reykjanes Peninsula, the weather was typical of Iceland, with the sun, rain, and everything in between all on the same day.

Reykjanes coast in August

If there is one conclusion to be reached from my experience visiting Iceland in different seasons, it is that the weather is always unexpected in Iceland. On top of that, everything changes rapidly so you should assume the worst and hope for the best, and be adaptable in case you need to adjust your plans.

Here you can discover our packing suggestions for Iceland for the winter months and here – Iceland packing ideas for the summer. Travel properly prepared and you will adore Iceland in every season and any weather!

Of course, traveling in summer or in winter would, in theory, provide you with radically different sensations. And things you will be able to see and experience all year long, some others are season-specific. Below, you can read an overview of the key advantages of visiting Iceland in each season to help you determine when is the ideal time for you to come to Iceland.

Just to be clear, by summer I mean June through August, and winter — October through April. May and September might be a little of both. Remember that you may experience summer AND winter in one day in any season in Iceland.

Activities you can do and locations you may visit in Iceland all year

The following locations and activities in Iceland are simple to visit the entire year-round:

Reykjavik (don't miss Perlan), Golden Circle (Thingvellir National Park, Gullfoss, Geysir), and the Southern coast of Iceland, all the way up to Jökulsárlón, may be visited all year. You may simply visit all these destinations with scheduled trips from Reykjavik in any season.

Natural spas such as Blue Lagoon, Sky Lagoon, and many more, as well as endless swimming pools, are all available all year round.

Glacier hiking, certain snowmobile trips, horseback riding - these and some other things you may perform in all seasons. There is also a natural ice cave – Katla – that you can explore the full year-round (all others – only in winter) (all others – only in winter).

Iceland is also a great photographer's paradise in any season. If you enjoy vacation photography, Iceland will provide you so many unique options for beautiful images.

Glacier trekking in Iceland may be done in any season

Advantages of visiting Iceland in summer

Here are several primary benefits of visiting Iceland in summer:

The days are long in Iceland in summer. In reality, they are boundless, so you may do much more touring.

It is warmer and dryer.

You can view some fauna. Theoretically speaking, you can see whales in any season, although the odds are substantially greater in summer. Puffins and most other birds can only be spotted in the summer months.

Roads are more accessible and you may travel to locations that are absolutely out of reach in winter.

Fully exploring the highlands in Iceland is only feasible in summer.

Many waterfalls are more accessible in summer. In winter you frequently have to view them from a safe distance since it's simply too slippery to approach closer.

The northern section of the island may be accessed easier in the summer months than in winter. The same goes for the Westfjords; sites like Dynjandi or Raudisandur are best visited in the summer months.

You may do the full Ring Road of Iceland without having to worry about driving conditions.

Camping is more pleasurable in summer. Here you may discover more information on camping in Iceland.

Some hiking can be done all year, but you will have many more alternatives in summer.

Most museums outside of Reykjavík are only open during the busy season.

Here you may discover a few examples of activities, excursions, and day trips you can do in Iceland in summer.

Puffin atop a cliff at a seashore in Southern Iceland
The southern coast of Iceland is the greatest area to observe puffins in summer

Advantages of visiting Iceland in winter

Here are the key benefits of visiting Iceland in winter:

Winter provides the most gorgeous light for photography. The days are shorter and your touring time is restricted, but the light is spectacular since the sun is so low on the horizon that it appears like sunset all day long.

Northern lights. The greatest time to observe Aurora Borealis in Iceland is from September to the beginning of April. In reality, there are only three conditions that decide whether you get to view the auroras: it needs to be dark, the sky has to be clear, and it helps if aurora activity is strong. Make sure you check aurora prediction websites to assist you in 'hunting' Northern lights. Even if the activity is minimal, you can typically see some auroras on a clear night, and a level 4 or 5 aurora show may be quite brilliant. Take a look at our beginners' guide to Northern Lights photography.

You may view the most spectacular frozen nature masterpieces in winter. Frozen waterfalls are amazing!

The most magnificent natural ice caves (around Skaftafell or at Jokulsarlon) may only be explored in the harshest winter months. They are beneath the water for the remainder of the year. Here you may get additional inspiration: bucket list-worthy winter adventures in Iceland.

Skiing, snowmobiling, and ice fishing are highly popular in the winter months. Although, as previously indicated, some snowmobile trips operate the full year-round.

There are fewer visitors in winter, therefore, it is less crowded attractions.

Prices of lodging and vehicle hire are reduced as well.

TIP: If you are still not sure when is the ideal time to visit Iceland, I may just have a great solution for you. I suggest visiting Iceland in September, particularly if it's your first trip.

One thing I know for sure — no matter which season you select, you will adore Iceland!

Must try Food in Iceland

Why Food Tasting Will Be The Best Part Of Your Iceland Trip

Discovering new cuisines and never-before-encountered sensations will open your eyes and your taste buds to a whole new spectrum of real flavors and recipes. Some of the most wonderful experiences imaginable await you here in Iceland! The Icelandic diet is among the healthiest in the world. The crystal clear water and air, the freely grazing sheep and cows, the wild fish, and the chemical-free vegetables form wonderful ingredients for what may be the highest quality meal you have ever had.

As an essential component, a country's cuisine is not only about its tastes but also talks about its culture and history. This is particularly true for Iceland! Getting to know the traditional cuisine is to learn about Icelandic history in the most thrilling way: via your senses.

The greatest thing is that you can sample most of these delicacies and explore Iceland's most renowned natural beauties on the Golden Circle Route on just one spectacular day tour: the Golden Circle Local Food Tour! Let us show you the most intriguing and the most unusual Icelandic cuisine that you must taste while visiting Iceland.

Verði þér að góðu - Enjoy your lunch!

SKYR - THE ICELANDIC YOGURT
Skyr is a pretty well-known Icelandic product. It has been a component of Icelandic cuisine for over a thousand years. Skyr is a cultured dairy product having the consistency of yogurt. It is quite similar to Greek yogurt, however, the taste is milder.

Icelanders commonly consume skyr with milk and fruit or berries, but it is also popular to use it in smoothies, ice cream, and in 'skyrkaka', a lighter and more popular alternative to cheesecake. Technically, Skyr is a soft cheese yet it is usually perceived as a yogurt.

Recently Skyr has been gaining popularity in other nations, and it is becoming more and more noticeable in grocery shops in places such as the United States and England.

SLOW ROASTED LAMB
Icelandic sheep are one of the purest breeds in the world. They have grazed on the slopes of Iceland ever since the first inhabitants brought them to this nation in the 9th century.

Lambs in Iceland are not fed on grain or given growth hormones. They travel freely outdoors from Spring to Autumn, consequently, their food is totally natural, consisting of grass, sedge, moss campion, and berries. The flesh of the Icelandic sheep is commonly regarded to be a gourmet meat, it is one of Iceland's best and most regularly used culinary items. Lamb very commonly occurs on celebratory meal menus or on Christmas Day.

The traditional technique to prepare a leg of lamb in Iceland is to roast it in the oven on a low fire for several hours, adding fresh herbs, notably blóðberg (Arctic thyme) to the flesh. The really Icelandic approach was to cook it for several hours in a geothermally heated pit in the earth!

Nowadays, preparing a great leg of lamb could not be easier, sprinkle your preferred fresh herbs and seasoning (marjoram, oregano, basil, sage, parsley, garlic, salt, and pepper) on a 2.2 - 2.5 kg) leg of lamb and set it into an oven that has been prepared to 200° C. After 30 to 40 minutes decrease the temperature to 180° C and cook it for a further 60 to 75 minutes, depending on how well done you want it.

The higher temperature sears the skin when you turn down the heat, you should check on the meat from time to time and cover it with foil or a lid if the skin is getting too crisp, or the herbs are singeing. Individual ovens vary so keep a watch on things!

If you want to prepare lamb fast simply purchase lamb fillet, which you can cook in 30 to 40 minutes at 200° C - you can even buy lamb fillet which is already marinated if you wish.

HÁKARL - FERMENTED SHARK

Hákarl is a typical meal in Iceland. Shark flesh has been cured using a special fermentation method, then hung outdoors to dry for four to five months. It has a very strong ammonia smell and a characteristic fishy flavor.

Hákarl is commonly served as cubes on cocktail sticks. First-timers are encouraged to pinch their noses when taking their first mouthful, the scent is much greater than the taste! After your first mouthful, do what the Icelanders do and have a big drink or two of the native spirit, brennivín, a sort of aquavit, frequently referred to as Icelandic schnapps.

Today, the fermented shark is not a meal that is regularly consumed by the natives. Most individuals who try it believe that it is very disgusting. Icelanders used to consume hákarl back in the day when they did not have refrigeration or many other food alternatives. Even while this meal isn't always the tastiest, it is a typical local delicacy that is distinctive of Iceland - something that you must eat when you travel to Iceland.

ICELANDIC LAMB SOUP - KJÖTSÚPA
Lamb soup is an Icelandic dish. It is becoming increasingly popular amongst

travelers and it has been consumed in Iceland for generations.

This creamy, flavorful soup is the ideal comfort meal for a long, gloomy winter's day. Each family has its unique recipe but traditional Icelandic meat soup is prepared with lamb shank or shoulder, potatoes, rutabagas (swede), and carrots. It may also include leeks, onions, dried herbs, salt, and pepper.

ICELANDIC FISH
Iceland has a large variety of fish on offer, over 340 species of saltwater fish have been reported in Icelandic waters. The most frequent saltwater fish are:

Wolffish/Atlantic Catfish
Capelin
Cod
Dealfish
Greenland shark
Haddock

Halibut
Lumpsucker or lumpfish
Lycodes
Mackerel
Monkfish
Saithe/Pollock

Three salmon species may be found in the rivers and lakes:

Arctic char
Atlantic salmon
Brown trout

You should aim to consume as much Icelandic fish as possible while you are in Iceland. Not only is it highly healthy for your health, but it also tastes delicious! In many places, you may have fish that was caught earlier that day, simply search for the 'fish of the day option on the menu. It doesn't get much fresher than that!

ICELANDIC HOT DOG

You may have previously heard of the legendary Icelandic Hot Dog. This commonplace foodstuff has garnered international notoriety over the years, Bill Clinton once famously declared them "the finest hot dogs in the world".

The Baejarins Beztu Pylsur is Iceland's most popular and most attended 'restaurant'. There is typically a large queue of people wanting to consume this delicacy. Despite their renown, these hot dogs are entirely reasonable, so do not miss the chance to have a hot dog when you visit Iceland!

RÚGBRAUÐ - DARK RYE BREAD FROM A HOT SPRING

Rúgbrauð is a traditional rye bread that Icelanders have been consuming for many years. It is either prepared in a pot or steamed in specific wooden barrels which have been placed in the ground near a hot spring.

This bread is crustless, dark brown, and substantial and its flavor is rather sweet. It is wonderful with butter, smoked salmon mutton pâté, hangikjöt (smoked lamb), or with pickled herring or cheese. Icelanders commonly eat this bread as a side dish with the Icelandic fish dish, plokkfiskur. You can get this bread at most grocery shops in Iceland.

HARÐFISKUR - DRIED FISH
Harðfiskur (which literally means hard fish) is an Icelandic dish that most locals appreciate. It may seem awful to many tourists, yet it is Iceland´s favorite food. Locals eat it with salted butter while watching a movie. It is regarded to be a healthier alternative to chips or popcorn.

Harðfiskur has been part of Icelandic cuisine for millennia. Most typically it is prepared with cod, although haddock or wolffish may also be utilized. It is dried in the cold North Atlantic air until it gets cured by microorganisms, the process is similar to maturing cheese.

Many people eat fish without anything on it, as a nutritious high-protein snack, while others prefer to eat it with lots of butter on it. You should absolutely try it!

BAKERY FOOD
If you travel to Iceland, you should make sure you have a brief visit to a local bakery. Iceland offers numerous excellent bakery dishes that you should try. The Icelandic snúður is a soft cinnamon bun, generally with an icing topping.

Kleina is a highly famous Scandinavian pastry, arguably the most popular pastry in Iceland. Bakeries are an economical alternative while dining out in Iceland, and their goods are, for certain, wonderful!

ICELANDIC ICE CREAM

Icelanders are enamored with ice cream. It doesn't matter whether it is winter or summer, frost might even add to the experience. You will see it for sale at many petrol stations, in most of the cafés, and there are also some great specialized ice cream stores across the nation.

Some ice cream parlors remain open till 1 am, so consumers may enjoy their ice cream at night too. There is an unusually extensive assortment of ice creams with many various toppings and sauces. Make sure you put Icelandic ice cream on your bucket list!

23 Absolute-Best Places to Visit in Iceland (+Things to Do & Tips)

While the list currently comprises more than the first top 10 sites, it does not list every single attraction or monument individually. We also didn't include all the facts regarding everything that you can do in Iceland.

The purpose of this part is to provide you with an overview of the most attractive regions, the finest activities to do, and the prettiest sites in Iceland that are worth visiting the most. So that you have a solid notion of where to visit in Iceland without becoming too overwhelmed with all the specifics.

Find out!

Without further ado, here is a list of the top locations to visit in Iceland:

1. Jökulsárlón Glacier Lagoon

Jökulsárlón Glacier Lagoon is not a coincidence the first one listed on this list. If there is one spot that you absolutely don't want to miss in Iceland, then it's Jokulsarlon.

The glacier lagoon is really magnificent and the view changes all the time. Icebergs shift all the time and no two visits are ever the same. In addition to the lagoon itself, you should also visit the so-called Diamond Beach, just over the road. When the weather conditions are good, you may view the most spectacular ice structures spread all over the beach. Shining in the sunshine like big diamonds...

For me, this beach is even more amazing than the lagoon itself. Especially on a beautiful winter day or around sunset. Magical!

TIP: You may want to check out the neighboring Fjallјökull glacial lagoon as well. It's smaller and less touristy than Jökulsárlón, and it's really wonderful too. Nearby Stokksnes beach is also well worth a visit.

How to visit: You may observe the Jokulsarlon glacier lagoon from land, or take a boat excursion (May-Oct) between the icebergs. You may select between an amphibious boat or a zodiac trip.

2. South Coast – Vík Beaches

Iceland's South Coast is one of the most frequented places in the nation and deservedly so. This region is really amazing!

The lovely settlement of Vik and the surrounding Reynisfjara beach and the spectacular coastline is well worth coming in any season. Vik black sand beach was formerly recognized as one of the ten most beautiful non-tropical beaches in the world.

TIP: Don't miss the adjacent Dyrhólaey Lighthouse and the beautiful rock formations seen from there.

How to visit: There are various parking sites along the shore near Vik. You'll need a vehicle to get here. Alternatively, you may visit on a South Coast trip from Reykjavik.

Important! Be Highly cautious on this beach — the waves here are unpredictable and it's very unsafe to stroll near the ocean. Even if the water seems calm, remain as far away as you can. Under no circumstances get into the water at Reynisfjara beach!

3. Golden Circle

By far the most popular area to visit in Iceland is the so-called Golden Circle. The

Golden Circle, historically also known as the Golden Triangle, refers to three major destinations - Thingvellir National Park, Gullfoss waterfall, and Geysir region with a particularly active Strokkur geyser.

Thingvellir National Park is most renowned for its continental divide, the Mid-Atlantic Ridge. It's a spot where you can see the opening between the tectonic plates of Europe and North America. It's a great location to explore on foot. Don't miss the slightly inconspicuous Öxarárfoss waterfall.

Gullfoss, or The Golden Waterfall, is one of the most beautiful waterfalls in Iceland. Must see!

You simply cannot travel to Iceland and not witness a geyser explode! The Geysir area is a geothermal region where the mother of all geysers - Geysir — is situated. While Geysir hasn't been active in a long time, there is a smaller geyser named Strokkur that erupts at regular intervals every 5-10 minutes. So you never have to wait long in order to view it.

TIP: While incredibly touristic, the Golden Circle is popular for a reason. If you can, arrive early in the morning or late in the evening in order to escape the greatest crowds.

How to visit: You'll need a vehicle to tour the Golden Circle. Alternatively, there are dozens of planned Golden Circle trips from Reykjavik.

4. Snaefellsnes Peninsula

Somewhat less frequented than the above-stated sites, Snæfellsnes Peninsula is another destination that you absolutely should see in Iceland. This is one of the spots that you can very readily in all seasons.

Best renowned for its magnificent Kirkjufell mountain and Kirkjufellsfoss waterfall, this region has so much more to offer than that! Volcanic landscapes, rocky coasts, amazing rock formations, innumerable waterfalls, lovely beaches, colorful lighthouses, charming small towns, and little attractive churches... These are just a few of the reasons to visit Snaefellsnes.

TIP: If you are going in summer and have the time, I suggest at least 2 days for this region.

How to visit: You'll need a vehicle to get around. Alternatively, take one of the guided Snaefellsnes day trips from Reykjavik.

5. Blue Lagoon

The Blue Lagoon is Iceland's most famous tourist destination and is regarded as the no. 1 must-visit location in Iceland. It's a gigantic outdoor geothermal pool with a characteristic blue or milky blue tint and very mild temps.

Good to know: Blue Lagoon is incredibly popular thus it's vital to secure your tickets in advance. You may book tickets here.

How to visit: Blue Lagoon is situated near Reykjavik KEF airport and you can either travel there by automobile or by taking a Blue Lagoon bus transfer from Reykjavik. It takes around an hour to travel there from the city and you will probably spend at least 2 hours in the water, so anticipate at least 4 hours for your stay.

TIP: You may also visit the Blue Lagoon on your route to or from the airport. Bus transfers are provided for Keflavik airport as well (see the link above) (see the link above).

Alternative: Instead of visiting Blue Lagoon (or in addition to it), you may prefer to visit the beautiful geothermal pool at Sky

Lagoon. It's situated in Reykjavik, considerably closer to town, and provides beautiful sea views and a unique Spa routine.

6. Skógafoss & Seljalandsfoss Waterfalls

These are the most popular waterfalls in Iceland after Gullfoss. The South Coast's Skógafoss and Seljalandsfoss are two must-see attractions in Iceland.

Skogafoss is a wonderfully spectacular waterfall. It's so photogenic that if you ever see images of a waterfall in Iceland, it's most likely to be Skogafoss. You may even climb the steps to the top of the waterfall for some wonderful views of the region.

Seljalandsfoss is the only Icelandic waterfall that I know of where you may walk behind the cascading water. In the winter, the waterfall is partly frozen and the entire area surrounding it appears like an ice skating rink, therefore the trail behind it is generally blocked. It's still pleasant to see and worth a quick stop. But it's most wonderful when you can stroll behind this waterfall and appreciate how beautiful this spot is. Prepare to get drenched!

TIP: Don't miss the secret Gljúfrabúi waterfall situated within the gorge only a short walk from Seljalandsfoss. It takes only a few minutes to visit — follow the trail to the left from Seljalandsfoss and you'll notice interpretive panels on the right side.

7. Myvatn

Myvatn Lake in the North of Iceland is another spot you absolutely should see in Iceland. This location is quite diversified and has a lot to offer, particularly in the warmer season.

Here are some of the greatest things to do at Myvatn: a stroll to the caldera of Krafla volcano and the lava fields, a short walk to the pseudocraters at Myvatn Lake, Leirhnjukur hiking route, Dimmuborgir region with spectacular lava structures and the 45-minute trek to Kirkjan lava tube complex.

Námaskarð geothermal region is also a must-see in North Iceland! It's a readily accessed small region with boiling mud pools and vivid steaming geothermal features. You have to be ready for the scent, however.

Myvatn Nature Baths are also not to be missed. This geothermal pool provides spectacular vistas, yet it's less congested and cheaper than the Blue Lagoon. However, it's evolved a lot in recent years, and so if you visit here in summer, anticipate it to be quite crowded. You may wish to reserve your tickets in advance here too!

How to visit: You'll need a vehicle to travel to Myvatn. If you are stopping at Akureyri on a cruise ship, you may see Myvatn on this popular shore excursion.

8. Húsavík

Known as the greatest site to observe whales in Iceland, Húsavík undoubtedly merits a mention as one of the top places to visit in Iceland as well. If you are visiting Northern Iceland in summer, whale viewing in Husavik is a must.

The town is really attractive also and you may visit the Húsavík Whale Museum. Another well-liked trend is geosea or geothermal sea baths.

TIP: Many whale-watching tours run from Husavik, but they're extremely popular and have to be booked in advance. One of the finest alternatives I constantly hear people mention is this trip with Gentle Giants.

9. Westfjords Region

If you want to venture a little off the beaten road in Iceland and experience some of its most spectacular, huge landscapes, then you certainly should consider visiting the Westfjords area.

It's fairly far away from anything, however, distances are huge, and most routes are gravel. So it's preferable to visit here in summer and arrive properly equipped.

The Dynjandi waterfall, the most stunning waterfall in Iceland, the Látrabjarg bird cliffs, the greatest site to see puffins in the summer, the endless red sand Rauisandur beach, and Safjörur town are just a few of the most amazing places not to be missed in the Westfjords.

You'll need at least 2-3 days to explore the full area and it will be hurried, but you can also see the key sites in 1-2 days.

How to visit: The Westfjords require 4WD or 4x4 vehicles. Check to see if driving on gravel roads is covered by your vehicle insurance.

TIP: The simplest method to travel to the Westfjords is by boarding a vehicle ferry from Stykkishólmur on Snaefellsnes Peninsula. That way, you may also only visit for one or two days and see the sights on the southern side of the Westfjords area.

10. Skaftafell National Park

Skaftafell NP is one of the easiest-accessible and scenic National Parks in Iceland. It, thus, merits a mention on any list of the top locations to see in Iceland.

There are numerous small hiking paths in this park. The most famous climb is that of Svartifoss — a waterfall flanked by stunning black basalt columns.

If you have a few hours to spare, try the Svartifoss – Sjónarsker – Sel hike and the trek to the glacier Skaftafellsjökull. Alternatively, the Svartifoss - Sjónarnípa trek is considerably longer but much more magnificent.

How to visit: Skaftafell NP is situated just off the Ring Road in the south of Iceland. You can simply travel here with a standard automobile. There is a Visitors' Center where you can additional information and acquire thorough hiking maps.

11. Icelandic Highlands

The greatest region of Iceland has virtually any roads and is relatively seldom visited, yet if there is one section of Iceland that is worth seeing more than anything else, it's the Icelandic Highlands!

Since the highlands are so large and there are so many wonderful hidden jewels, it would be hard to list even a tiny fraction of them. At the same time, most sites are highly isolated and need local expertise and super jeeps with enormous tires to access them... Furthermore, the highlands are only accessible from around mid-June until mid-September.

Some of my favorite sites in the highlands that are reasonably simple to visit include Kerlingarfjöll, Háifoss, and Landmannalaugar. Haifoss waterfall is relatively simple to see on your own as well.

How to visit: You'll need a decent 4WD or a 4×4 for all of the destinations described above, but the simplest way to visit is by taking a tour. If you want to get a flavor of what the highlands are like, the most popular highlands trips are those to Landmannalaugar.

12. Reykjanes Peninsula

One of the simplest sites to visit in Iceland from our list, the Reykjanes Peninsula is typically ignored by most Iceland visitors. Their loss! This gorgeous region adjacent to Keflavik airport and Reykjavik city is home to the famed Blue Lagoon and is well worth a visit too.

With colorful geothermal zones, vast lava fields, and breathtaking craggy coasts, Reykjanes Peninsula is like the best of Iceland in a nutshell.

Don't miss the Valahnúkamöl Cliffs near Reykjnesviti Lighthouse and Seltún Geothermal Area. Bridge Between Continents is another lovely place, just like Strandarkirkja and Garður. Krysuvikurberg

Cliffs are incredibly stunning also but need a 4 WD vehicle to reach there.

How to visit: You may easily explore most of the sights of the Reykjanes Peninsula by yourself with a conventional automobile. Alternatively, take one of the guided trips from Reykjavik. Some spots demand a 4WD or perhaps a super jeep.

13. Recently-Active Volcanos

This is the newest addition to the finest things to do in Iceland — trekking to one of the recently-erupted volcanos!

In March 2021, there was an eruption of the Fagradalsfjall volcano on the Reykjanes Peninsula. The surrounding Geldingadalir valley was filled with blazing lava and the panorama was changing frequently. The volcano swiftly became the new most popular attraction in Iceland drawing residents and visitors alike.

At the time of the previous update, these volcanic outbursts had ended. But the eruption sites remain a highly popular spot to view in Iceland, bringing millions of people every day.

Good to know: The simplest method to travel to volcanic eruption locations is by automobile or by taking a tour. There are quite a few volcanic trips offered. They include pick-up/ drop-off in Reykjavik and some additionally visit a couple of the key sights of the Reykjanes Peninsula or include tickets to the Blue Lagoon.

14. Tröllaskagi Peninsula

If there is one region in North Iceland that appears to be utterly disregarded by foreign visitors, it's the magnificent town of Siglufjörður and its surrounds, nicknamed the Tröllaskagi Peninsula. It's really amazing!

The fishermen's village Siglufjörður is quite lovely and The Herring Era Museum is definitely worth a visit. But maybe even more spectacular is the picturesque trip to get there. Road 76 which travels from Varmahlíð to Siglufjörður is undoubtedly the most magnificent scenic drive in Iceland.

TIP: Make sure to stop at Hofsós bathing pool. Don't miss the Grafarkirkja (supposed to be the oldest church in Iceland)! Víðimýrarkirkja and Glaumbaer Farm & Museum are well worth a visit.

How to visit: You'll need a vehicle to explore this region.

15. Heimaey Island

Part of Iceland's Westman Islands, Heimaey Island is the largest island and one of the most beautiful spots in Iceland.

It's a location where you can become familiar with the more traditional style of life in Iceland and experience what it's actually like to live on a distant island. Especially if you visit outside the peak season.

The scenery here is spectacular, and in summer, you may see hundreds of puffins on the island. There is also a whale sanctuary where you may watch white Beluga whales.

How to visit: You'll need to take a boat to get here. Private tours from Reykjavik are also available, but quite pricey. For comparison, make sure to check this option as well — the rates depend on your group size.

16. Dettifoss & Asbyrgi

There are two additional spots in Northern Iceland that are well worth seeing and deserve a mention among the greatest things to do in Iceland - Dettifoss Waterfall and Asbyrgi Canyon.

Dettifoss is Europe's most powerful waterfall. With 100 meters (330 ft) in width, a drop of 44 meters (144 ft), and an average water flow of 193 m^3/s, this is the site where you experience the force of nature like nowhere else in Iceland. Must watch!

Asbyrgi Canyon is a relatively lesser-known area situated between Dettifoss and Husavik and it's definitely worth a brief stop or a longer stay. It always fascinates me how entirely diverse landscapes can be so near to one other and the calm of Asbyrgi is absolutely incomparable to the roaring strong Dettifoss.

How to visit: Road #862 to Dettifoss is paved and reasonably accessible (road #864 is not and needs a 4WD). Road #861 to Asbyrgi is also paved. However, road #862 north of Dettifoss is gravel and it's better to have a 4WD if you are going to travel here. Alternatively, you may reach Asbyrgi from Husavik.

17. Vatnajökull Glacier

With so many glaciers in Iceland, it's hard to select just one to list as the finest one to see. However, Vatnajökull Glacier is the greatest ice cap in Iceland. So if you visit only one glacier in Iceland, it will likely be this one.

With a total size of +- 7,900 km2 (3,100 sq mi), Vatnajokull is vast. It contains roughly 30 glacier tongues (outlet glaciers), each with its own name, and therefore it's probable that you'll find their names stated in the description of different glacier excursions and activities.

How to visit: You can observe different glacier tongues from the Ring Road in southern Iceland. But the greatest way to explore glaciers in Iceland is by arranging a glacier hiking trip, exploring the ice caves, and snowmobiling. Keep in mind that you need to schedule an organized tour for any activities where you go on the glacier itself.

In winter – from roughly October to March – you may also visit some of the most magnificent natural ice caves in Iceland. You may only visit on a tour and you should reserve in advance. There is also one spot – Katla – where you may see a natural ice cave in the summer as well. This is the greatest trip that travels to Katla ice cave and it leaves from Vik. There is also a day excursion that explores this ice cave from Reykjavik.

18. East Fjords

Another place that is typically ignored by people who only drive the Ring Road from South to North is the East Fjords. It's a gorgeous place that is definitely worth seeing if you cross eastern Iceland!

The loveliest towns are probably Eskifjörður and Seyðisfjörður, the latter is noted for its bright rainbow road leading to the church. In season, Borgarfjörður Eystri is a nice site to watch puffins.

There are also hundreds of waterfalls in the vicinity, hiking routes, Laugarfell hot spring, and Petra's Stone collection near Stöðvarfjörður...

The eastern portion of Iceland is where you're most likely to observe reindeer.

How to visit: You will need a vehicle to see the East Fjords.

19. Fjaðrárgljúfur Canyon

Fjaðrárgljúfur Canyon near Kirkjubaejarklaustur used to be one of my favorite spots in Iceland. It was so serene and unknown. Nowadays, it's so popular that the walking trail along the edge of the canyon had to be blocked so that nature could recover a little.

There are other really gorgeous canyons in Iceland, but this one is the simplest to visit. So if you want to see a canyon in Iceland, Fjaðrárgljúfur is definitely worth a trip. Just please be courteous to nature and heed the signs.

How to visit: You'll need a vehicle to get here. This Jokulsarlon day excursion includes stops at Fjadrargljufur.
Fjadrargljufur Canyon is one of the must-visit locations in Iceland

20. Goðafoss Waterfall

One of the most popular waterfalls in Northern Iceland is Goafoss, which refers to "the waterfall of the Gods."

It's incredibly gorgeous and particularly on a bright day. Often, you may see a rainbow above the falls and it looks just amazing.

How to visit: Located immediately next to the Ring Road, Godafoss is quite simple to travel to by automobile. All North Iceland trips that visit Myvatn stop here as well. Paved walking routes joined by a pedestrian bridge enable you to observe the waterfall from two sides of the river.

21. Hvitserkur

Hvitserkur is a stunning rhino-shaped rock near the northern shore of Iceland. While the rock itself is really stunning, the whole region surrounding it is just magnificent.

We were not sure whether it was worth the lengthy travel, but it surely is. I, therefore, believe that Hvitserkur deserves to be considered among the most beautiful spots in Iceland. If you are traveling in the north anyhow, this is merely a relatively short diversion from the Ring Road.

How to visit: You'll need a vehicle to get here. The road is gravel but in fair shape.

22. Reykjavík

While I believe that Iceland's beauty rests largely in its landscape and people rather than its towns, no list of the greatest locations in Iceland would be complete without including its capital city, Reykjavik.

Reykjavik has altered beyond recognition in the last few years and it has more to offer to visitors than ever before.

In the past, I would have told you that one day is more than enough to see all the highlights, which include the views from Hallgrimskirkja church tower, discovering the streets of the colorful town center, feeding ducks at the Reykjavik Lake Tjörnin, visiting Harpa concert hall, seeing the Sun Voyager statue, and visiting some museums.

However, there is now so much more to see and do in Reykjavik than that, with new spectacular attractions popping up all across the city all the time. So if you do have some additional time to spare, schedule a few days in Reykjavik

TIP: My favorite museum that I highly suggest in Reykjavik is Perlan. Here you can discover our guide to Perlan, the greatest museum in Reykjavik.

Other fantastic attractions are FlyOver Iceland, Whales of Iceland, Magic Ice Bar, and the geothermal pool with cliffside ocean views, Sky Lagoon.

23. Akureyri

For those of you who are wondering why Akureyri is at the bottom of this list... While I think that it's a lovely site to stop for an hour or two if you have lots of time in Iceland, I also feel that there are so many prettier places to visit in North Iceland that are worth your time.

That being said, if you travel to Akureyri, don't miss the Botanical Gardens. There are also several excellent locations to explore nearby, so you could use Akureyri as a 'base' point for exploring more of Northern Iceland.

If you are simply traveling through, you may wish to stop by the Christmas House just outside of town.

So, this is our guide to some of the very greatest spots to see in Iceland.

I hope that it will encourage you to explore this wonderful nation beyond its most famous tourist sites like the Golden Circle, Reykjavik, and the South Coast.

Grand Golden Circle Day Trips in Iceland

The Golden great Circle trip brings one to Iceland's southwest portions and the notable sites that are a part of it. The location provides some of the most breathtaking vistas. Usually, the departure for the excursion takes place from the city of Reykjavik. The duration of the voyage is seven hours roughly. With the tour providers, you will have stops at some of the important locations. There are National; Parks where you may observe the Eurasian and American plates. These plates are observed to be coming apart, and several other major attractions. These include Gullfoss Waterfall which is also touted to be Europe's most powerful waterfall ranking second. You will also come across the geothermal region of Geysir. The operators frequently arrange for additional stops in some of the most renowned places. Details of the places are listed below.

National Park

The Grand Golden Circle day vacations are never complete without a visit to the National Park of Thingvellir. It is not simply a location that is regarded as a marvel geologically but has layers of history. This waterfall is situated at the meeting point of the Eurasian and North American plates. The location of Thingvellir is an old one where the first parliament of the world was established and the assembly is conducted every year, outdoors. The whole of it lasted up through 1798, commencing from 930 AD. This location recounts tales of political, and geographical battles, continual development, and compromises. Hence, in the year 2004, it was smoothly placed on the global Heritage list UNESCO.

Geothermal area and waterfall

If you are starting with the Grand Golden Circle day tours then the tour operators are obliged to take you to the geothermal region of Geysir and the stunning waterfall of Gullfoss. After the national Park, Geysir is the next destination. This is the area you may watch the explosion of geysers right before your eyes. Geysir unexpectedly ceased erupting during the early era of the 2000s although Strokkur touted as the "baby brother" goes off now and then. The third stop is the stunning falls of Gullfoss that dips down in stages twenty-one meters and eleven meters before it falls into a fissure thus, vanishing later in the soil. The waterfall may be admired from numerous beautiful spots.

Kerio and Faxi
The fourth stop of the tour should be a waterfall named the waterfall of Faxi. This specific fall is situated in the Tungufljot River and the drop is seven meters below. It is noted for its vast width of eighty meters. Another thing that is unique about the falls is that you shall discover tonnes of fish here. The fifth and last destination is a lake of a

volcanic crater named Great Kerio. This one is situated in southern Iceland. This specific lake is also termed the western zone of volcanic events. The zone contains the glacier of Langjokull and the Peninsula of Reykjanes.

Endless enjoyment assured
Venturing with this amazing vacation is likely to have a beneficial influence on your attitude since you are enrolling yourself on an everlasting voyage of joy. You are accompanied by an audio guide of English with a minibus as a conveyance. You shall be collected from and dropped off at your place of lodging. Make the most of the travel with complimentary Wi-Fi on board.

Some Secret Places Along Iceland's Golden Circle

Iceland is full of magnificent sights and great experiences. The tranquility of the nation is considered the greatest in the whole globe. Visitors will discover perfect peace within the abundant natural heritage and also have interesting travels every day.

A Golden Circle Tour is great to discover the majesty and magnificence of Iceland on a single visit. It is regarded to be one of the greatest sites to explore in the nation. The whole circle comprises magnificent historical attractions, hot springs, lagoons, volcanic vistas, and geysers. Here we'll go over the techniques via which one may enjoy the greatest golden circle tour in Iceland.

One may take a tour break at the volcanic island

This stop will improve the enjoyment of the whole journey. The volcanic island is one major tourist part as well. One may walk into the volcanic caverns and into the mouth where the molten remnants and black formations are intriguing to examine.

Adventure is probably boundless in such sections of the land.

Go check out the renowned Black Sand Beach

Our unusual site was sculpted totally by the forces of nature and is unlike anything on this globe. The collision of the European and North American tectonic plates in the adjoining areas of the continents has caused massive eruptions and volcanic activity in the past, ultimately leading to a dark gloomy form of rocks, gravel, and sand. Hence a beach was built with black sand as time advanced.

The waterfalls are spectacular

A trip will also include stops at the waterfalls surrounding the circle. Such areas are exceedingly tranquil and serve as the perfect place to unwind. Furthermore, the grandeur of the falls, position, and photogenic zones give abundant opportunities for guests to enjoy an experience of a lifetime.

One such place is the Gullfoss Falls which is a wonderful natural structure. The strong flow of water dominates the tranquillity of the location, altogether making it a joyful and quiet atmosphere to spend leisure excursions.

Have an experience in the National Park

Apart from mental serenity and physical rest in the serene locations of the circle, considerable adventure awaits the demands of tourists at the Thingvellir National Park. Visitors will enjoy a fantastic experience at this ancient location where rare ruins, preserved sculptures, and intriguing stone constructions are viewed. Hikers will appreciate the tranquil but exciting stroll which will be full of scenic beauty and unique wildlife encounters.

Manage your budget

Iceland could turn out to be pricey; yet, there are important approaches to reduce the economic constraints and experience a great vacation. Trip operators provide outstanding services to visitors, offering travel packages that are reasonable and easily encompass a broad variety of activities.

Furthermore, the personalized tour packages would enable guests to design a journey as per their interests at an affordable price. There are also internet ways to contact such agencies so that the individual may pick from the comfort of their own homes before beginning on the voyage.

What can be concluded?

The Golden Circle is surely a lovely spot to visit. It includes various stops that will take guests on a bizarre adventure. One will experience the grandeur of nature and beautiful vistas, altogether witnessing moments in life that may be remembered for a whole lifetime.

The best itineraries for Iceland from one day to two weeks

Are you seeking the ideal Iceland itinerary? This book covers all of the greatest Iceland itineraries, whether you are there for only one day or two weeks.

There is so much to see and do in Iceland from having a bath in natural hot springs to chasing waterfalls to trekking on a glacier! While a longer vacation to Iceland would be ideal, that's not always feasible and a short Iceland itinerary is essential instead. But regardless of the length of the Iceland itinerary, they are all filled with fantastic things to do!

To aid you with your Iceland vacation planning process, check out our advice on where to stay in Iceland. And if you intend on hiring a vehicle, be careful to avoid these seven Iceland car rental blunders.

How Many Days Should You Spend In Iceland?

Iceland is such a lovely nation loaded with so much to see and do. While any length of time in Iceland is fantastic, I suggest staying at least five days. But if you'd want to explore as much of the nation as possible, you'll need at least 10 days to see everything the region has to offer.

Getting Around During Your Iceland Itinerary

There are several various methods to travel about Iceland, such as a rented vehicle, public transport, or excursions. On shorter vacations, you may just take the public bus and excursions to view what you would want to see. There are so many fantastic Tours In Iceland that you may be interested in!

However, for longer excursions that will enable you to explore more off-the-beaten-path sections of Iceland, you should hire a vehicle or campervan.

We adore Driving In Iceland and strongly suggest it if you are prepared for exploring!

How These Iceland Itinerary Suggestions Were Determined

These Iceland itinerary options are precisely what I would propose to a family member or friend traveling to Iceland!

As you read on, you may note that Reykjavik, the capital of Iceland, isn't prominently included on this list. In my perspective, you travel to Iceland for nature and not the city, thus you'll see a lot more nature stops instead.

1 Day In Iceland Stopover Itinerary

If you just have one day in Iceland (for a layover, for example), this one-day Iceland itinerary is great, since you can still visit some of the most interesting things the nation has to offer! For a one-day layover, I strongly suggest lodging near the airport, since the airport is a 45-minute drive from Reykavik. Then, you can easily take a bus to Reykjavik instead.

If your Iceland schedule is restricted to only a day, you'll have to pick whether you wish to concentrate on nature or see the city.

1-Day Itinerary Option 1: Focus On Nature

Day 1: The Blue Lagoon And The Reykjanes Peninsula

To enjoy a piece of Iceland's nature during your one-day schedule, I suggest seeing the

Reykjanes Peninsula. While this does need a vehicle, car rentals in Iceland aren't too costly, particularly if you are spreading the cost amongst a big group of people.

At Reykjanes Peninsula, there are a ton of great natural areas to explore. Stop at Reykjanesviti, Iceland's oldest lighthouse. Then go over to the beautiful cliffs of Valahnukamol only feet away. Don't forget to see the bubbling Gunnuhver geothermal region, the natural ocean pool known as Brimketill, and the towering Hafnarberg cliffs.

This peninsula also happens to sit on the boundary between the tectonic plates of Europe and North America. There's a rift in the ground where these tectonic plates meet, and you can traverse a bridge, known as the Bridge between Continents, across it.

Last but not least, the Reykjanes Peninsula is home to Iceland's famed Blue Lagoon.

Take a break from your hectic one-day Iceland agenda and soak up the warmth.

1-Day Itinerary Option 2: Reykjavik And Blue Lagoon (Without A Car).

Day 1: Reykjavik And The Blue Lagoon

If you feel like you have to see Reykjavik during your day in Iceland, this Iceland itinerary choice is for you!

In the morning, visit the city of Reykjavik. See the Sun Voyager sculpture, shop downtown, look in marvel at the HARPA Center, tour a couple of the city's numerous museums, and check out the historic Hallgrimskirikja Church.

In the afternoon, leave the city and travel out into nature. Since you can't miss the Blue Lagoon, go relax in the warmth of this natural hot spring.

2 Days In Iceland Itinerary

While two days may seem a bit short, you can still experience so much of the beauty of Iceland in that 48 hours. If you have two days in Iceland, you may still visit the nation utilizing public buses and excursions. But if you'd want to plunge into the nature of Iceland over your two days, consider hiring a vehicle.

2 Day Suggestions Without A Car

Day 1: Reykjavik And Blue Lagoon

Day 2: The Golden Circle Or The South Coast

The first day of this two days in Iceland schedule is similar to the prior one-day Iceland trip plan. Visit Hallgrimskirikja

Church, the HARPA Center, and the Sun Voyager sculpture. Visit a couple of the city's many museums while shopping downtown. towering columned church in Reykjavik Iceland Itinerary

Then, after you've got your fill of the city, get on a trip to Iceland's famed Blue Lagoon.

The second day takes of this Iceland itinerary takes you further out of the capital. I propose taking a trip either to the Golden Circle or the South Coast.

The Golden Circle in Iceland is encrusted in diamonds. Thingvellir National Park, one of Iceland's finest national parks, is the most well-liked destination along this route. Thingvellir National Park is unmatched by any other place on earth due to its abundance of snow-covered lava rock and frequent appearances by the breathtaking Northern Lights. Other breathtaking sites near the Golden Circle are Kerid Crater,

Langjokull Glacier, Helgufoss Waterfall, and Thurofoss Waterfall.

If you'd like, you may substitute a trip to the Golden Circle for a tour of the South Coast. Rather than the two waterfalls of the Golden Circle, the South Coast boasts two waterfalls of its own: Seljalandsfoss and Skogafoss. These two waterfalls are among the finest things to view in South Iceland. Combine these waterfalls with a journey to the Sólheimajökull glacier and Reynisfjara black sand beach.

2-Day Suggestions With A Car

Day 1: Explore Reykjanes Peninsula

Day 2: The Golden Circle And Blue Lagoon

If you have a vehicle during your two days in Iceland, you have the option of traveling a little bit further out of the city: to the

Reykjanes Peninsula. This itinerary is identical to the last Reykjanes Peninsula: Stop to visit the Reykjanesviti lighthouse, the cliffs of Valahnukamol, and the Hafnarberf cliffs.

Then, you may travel for approximately an hour till you reach the Reykjadalur Hot Springs Thermal River. You'll have to trek a little less than an hour to reach this natural wonder, but it'll be worth it because it's one of Iceland's greatest hot springs.

The Golden Circle in Iceland may be driven alone rather than on a tour! As I said previously, the Golden Circle features magnificent stops, like Thingvellir National Park, Kerid Crater, Langjokull Glacier, Helgufoss Waterfall, and Thurofoss Waterfall.

Then, travel for approximately an hour till you reach Hrualog Hot Springs. This hot spring is very under-the-radar and is frequented more by locals than visitors. And since you just can't get enough of the hot springs in Iceland, the final visit on your Iceland itinerary is the Blue Lagoon!

3 Days In Iceland Itinerary

If you have three days in Iceland, the itineraries below will guarantee that your vacation is jam-packed with the incredible natural splendor of nature.

3 Day Iceland Itinerary Without A Car
Day 1: Reykjavik And Blue Lagoon

Day 2: The Golden Circle Or Snaefellsnes Peninsula Tour

Day 3: South Coast

Just like many of the other Iceland itineraries dependent on public transit and excursions, you may spend your first day in

Iceland exploring the city of Reykjavik and then take a trip to the famed Blue Lagoon.

The Golden Circle has made a few reappearances previously on this list because places like Thingvellir National Park and Kerid Crater just can't be missed.

As an option, you might take a tour of Snæfellsnes Peninsula instead. This peninsula offers so much to do, but it is most renowned for the towering Kirkjufell Mountain and the surrounding Kirkjufellsfoss.

Like the Golden Circle, the South Coast has shown up a few times in this Iceland itinerary guide a few times. Seljalandsfoss, Skogafoss, Sólheimajökull glacier, and Reynisfjara black sand beach are all excellent sites to view.

3 Day Iceland Itinerary With A Car

Day 1: The Golden Circle and the Blue Lagoon

Day 2: Hot Springs And Waterfalls

Day 3: South Coast

With a vehicle, you have a bit more freedom, so you may see both the Blue Lagoon and the Golden Circle on the first day of your Iceland itinerary. End your Golden Circle drive at Selfoss, so you'll be prepared for the following day's excursions.

Start the second day of your Iceland journey with not one, but TWO hot springs. First, go to Reykjadalur Hot Springs and then proceed to the under-the-radar Hrualog Hot Springs.

Then, you'll go to one of the greatest waterfalls in Iceland: Haifoss Waterfall. You'll likely have this tremendous 400-foot waterfall all to yourself since it is mainly inaccessible unless you have a 4×4. Despite the additional work it takes to get there, Haifoss Waterfall is worth it.

In between these magnificent parts of nature, make a visit to Þjóðveldisbærinn Saga-Age Farm for a little bit of history. Once upon a time, Þjóðveldisbærinn Saga-Age Farm was home to the remnants of a Viking village. Now you may view these same ruins and a restored farm fashioned like those of the historical period.

Leave the realm of the Vikings and visit a location that appears like it may be home to mythical fairies: Gjain. With gushing waterfalls, towering basalt columns, and vibrant vegetation, it's little surprise that people – including the stars of Game of Thrones – hurry to this magnificent place.

Finally, drive to Hella or the South Coast to rest before your third and final day.

Of course, I had to include the South Coast in my Iceland itinerary as well. Bottom line: add Skogafoss, Seljalandsfoss, Reynisfjara black sand beach, and Sólheimajökull glacier to your list of things to visit in Iceland. Don't forget to check out our advice for Solheimajokull Glacier!

4 Days In Iceland Itinerary

Day 1: The Golden Circle and the Blue Lagoon

Day 2: Hot Springs And Waterfalls

Day 3: South Coast

Day 4: The National Park of Skaftafell and the Glacier Lagoons

For the 4 days in Iceland plan, I would suggest completing the three days in Iceland itinerary with a vehicle indicated above. Then, on day four, drive to Skaftafell National Park and two glacier lagoons.

Skaftafell National Park features all various sorts of scenery – from glaciers to volcanoes to waterfalls – which means that there is so much to do and see. You may stroll to the waterfalls and glaciers, view Icelandic wildlife, and even enjoy an ice cave tour!
waterfall flanked by basalt columns Iceland Itinerary

Within an hour of Skaftafell National Park, two glacier lagoons are worth a visit: Jokulsarlon Glacier Lagoon and Fjallsarlon Glacier Lagoon. Both of these lagoons are lakes in the middle of enormous glaciers and are hidden beauties of Iceland.

As you float in the river, enormous pieces of glacier ice speckled with volcanic ash will drift past. There's absolutely nothing else like it. The best way to explore Jokulsarlon

Glacier Lagoon and Fjallsarlon Glacier Lagoon is on a boat excursion.

5 Days In Iceland Itinerary

Day 1: Hot Springs And Waterfalls

Day 2: South Coast

Day 3: The Glacier Lagoons and The National Park of Skaftafell

Day 4: Southeast Iceland

Day 5: Blue Lagoon And Reykjavik

During these five days in Iceland, you'll be able to visit some of the greatest things that Iceland has to offer, including hot springs, black sand beaches, and glaciers.

The same hot springs and waterfalls day from the three-day Iceland itinerary above are returning in this five days in Iceland plan! Head to the Reykjadalur Hot Springs and Hrualog Hot Springs, read about the history of the Vikings at Þjóðveldisbaerinn Saga-Age Farm, and take in the grandeur of the Haifoss Waterfall and the Gjain Valley. Then, spend the night at Hella or on the South Coast.

And the South Coast is returning! Be sure to check out all of the waterfalls, glaciers, and black sand beaches in the vicinity, as indicated in the preceding itinerary.

Skaftafell National Park and the surrounding glacier lagoons had to make a return as well. Take your time seeing the varied vistas of Skaftafell National Park before taking a boat excursion or two around Jokulsarlon Glacier Lagoon and Fjallsarlon Glacier Lagoon.

If you still have time, try making a trip to Diamond Beach as well. Located just across the street from Jokulsarlon Glacier Lagoon, Diamond Beach is one of the nicest black sand beaches in Iceland. Because it is so near to Jokulsarlon Glacier Lagoon, little ice crystals from the glacier end up on the beach and make it gleam as though it's strewn with diamonds.

On day four of your Iceland itinerary, you'll see Southeast Iceland, beginning with the awe-inspiring mountain peaks of Stokksnes. Then, travel to the Fjadrargljufur Canyon, one of the most stunning canyons in Iceland, where the vivid green moss, deep canyon fissures, and rushing river form a spectacular environment.

The final destination of the day is the Mulagljufur Canyon. You'll have to travel a mile and a half to reach the magnificent, under-the-radar canyon, but it'll be worth it. Along the route, you'll be surrounded by brilliant foliage and falling water before reaching the Hangandifoss and Mulafoss Waterfalls.

Then, proceed to go back down the South Coast towards Reykjavik.

Despite enjoying a couple of days on Iceland's South Coast, there may be a few activities that you just didn't have time for. Day 5 is the greatest opportunity to explore those attractions!

If you saw all that you wanted to, proceed to the famed Blue Lagoon. And if you still have time, try touring Reykjavik or the Reykjanes Peninsula.

6 Days in Iceland Itinerary

Day 1: Hot Springs And Waterfalls

Day 2: South Coast

Day 3: The Glacier Lagoons and The National Park of Skaftafell

Day 4: Southeast Iceland

Day 5: Blue Lagoon And Reykjavik

Day 6: The Westman Islands or the Snaefellnes Peninsula

For the six days in Iceland schedule, I would suggest finishing the five days in Iceland itinerary and then traveling to Snaefellsnes Peninsula or the Westman Islands.

The Snæfellsnes Peninsula, like most of Iceland, is packed with breathtaking scenery. If there are two things you must see on this peninsula, it is the majestic Kirkjufell Mountain and the adjacent Kirkjufellsfoss Waterfall.
brilliant green mountain bordered by the waterfall

As an alternative, you might go to the Westman Islands. These islands off the South Coast of Iceland may be the country's best-hidden secret. To go to the Westman Islands, you can either take a plane or a boat, however, I strongly suggest taking the ferry. Then, once there, there is so much to do! Check out the striking black Heimaey Stave Church, visit Stórhöfði (the southernmost point in Iceland) and look for puffins, or even take a boat tour of the islands!

7 Days In Iceland Itinerary

Day 1: Golden Circle and Hot Springs

Day 2: South Coast

Day 3: Westman Islands

Day 4: Skaftafell and Glacier Lagoons

Day 5: Southeast Iceland

Day 6: Snaefellsnes Peninsula

Day 7: The Blue Lagoon, Reykjavik, And The Reykjanes Peninsula

Congratulations! You get to spend an entire week in Iceland! And this seven days in Iceland schedule is jam-packed with nature and adventure.

Visit the spectacular views of the Golden Circle, including Thingvellir National Park, Kerid Crater, Langjokull Glacier, Helgufoss Waterfall, and Thurofoss Waterfall. Then, warm up in the Hrunalog and Reykjadalur Hot Springs.

Skogafoss, Seljalandsfoss, Reynisfjara black sand beach, and Sólheimajökull glacier should all be included in your Iceland South Coast itinerary.

Take a boat or aircraft to the Westman Islands, where you may explore the Heimaey Stave Church, Stórhöfði, and Eldfell Crater.

Skaftafell National Park, Jokulsarlon Glacier Lagoon, Fjallsarlon Glacier Lagoon, and Diamond Beach are all beautiful scenery. From waterfalls to glaciers to black sand beaches, this part of Iceland is incredibly varied.

Stare at the towering mountains of Stokksnes, take in the stunning environment of Fjadrargljufur Canyon, and climb to Mulagljufur Canyon before beginning to travel back in the direction of Reykjavik.

Be sure to view the Kirkjufell Mountain and Kirkjufellsfoss Waterfall when visiting the Snaefellsnes Peninsula.

Day 7 of our Iceland itinerary is a wonderful buffer day for you to check out anything from the previous days that you just did not have time for.

As an alternative, if you're on schedule, you may climb the Glymur Waterfall and Canyon. Know that this four-hour climb is tough for the novice or faint of heart. You'll need to hike over high cliffs, climb into caverns, and cross rivers. But if you're an explorer at heart, it'll all be worth it to view the 650-foot Glymur Waterfall.

If it sounds a bit too daring for your taste, you may explore the Reykjanes Peninsula or Reykjavik. At the Reykjanes Peninsula, visit Reykjanesviti, the cliffs of Valahnukamol, the Gunnuhver geothermal region, and the Brimketill ocean pool. In Reykjavik, check out the Sun Voyager sculpture the HARPA Center, the Hallgrimskirikja Church, and a couple of the museums.

Finish off your day with a peaceful dip in the Blue Lagoon.

10 Days In Iceland Itinerary - FULL RING ROAD!

Day 1: Hot Springs And Waterfalls

Day 2: Begin To Explore The South Coast

Day 3: Continue To Explore The South Coast

Day 4: Canyons And Skaftafell

Day 5: Southeast Iceland

Day 6: East Fjords

Day 7: Waterfalls And Whale Watching

Day 8: Northern Iceland

Day 9: Snaefellness Peninsula

Day 10: Reykjavik And The Blue Lagoon

One of the coolest things to do in Iceland is to tour the full of Iceland's ring road. Because this 828-mile journey is so extensive and has so much to see, I would not advocate taking the complete ring road tour unless you have ten days! While it can be done in a week, it's simply not as pleasurable and you will likely feel as if you're rushing through things. In other words, it's the ideal thing to do for 10 days in Iceland!

The first day of our Ring Road schedule may appear a bit familiar. Head to Reykjadalur Hot Springs, Hrualog Hot Springs, Haifoss Waterfall, Þjóðveldisbaerinn Saga-Age Farm, and Gjain before spending the night in Hella or on the South Coast.

For day two of your ten-day Iceland itinerary, start visiting the South Coast. Check out Skogafoss, Seljalandsfoss, and Reynisfjara black sand beach.

Your time touring Iceland's South Coast isn't done yet! While you've already visited the waterfalls and black sand beaches, there are also glaciers to explore. Visit Sólheimajökull glacier, Langjokull glacier, and Myrsdalsjokull glacier. To take a respite from all the glaciers, travel to Þakgil, a lovely green canyon in the heart of all of the freezing glaciers.

Explore the magnificent Fjadrargljufur Canyon and Mulagljufur Canyon. While Fjadrargljufur Canyon is pretty simple to get, you'll have to climb a little bit to Mulagljufur Canyon. That said, it's worth it since you'll witness the Hangandifoss and Mulafoss Waterfalls.

In addition to the two canyons, the fourth day of this Iceland itinerary also includes a visit to Skaftafell National Park, where you can enjoy a tour of an ice cave, get views of Icelandic wildlife, and trek to glaciers and waterfalls.

Southeast Iceland offers a range of varied landscapes. Sail around the Jokulsarlon and Fjallsarlon Glacier Lagoons, take in the majestic Stokksnes mountain peaks, and discover the black sand at Diamond Beach. couple on the reflected ground in front of towering mountains during golden hour

Southeast Iceland is also home to one of Iceland's best-hidden gems: a Viking hamlet film set. Wander through the tiny settlement with grass-thatched rooftops shielded by a steep high peak.

Then, make your way to the village of Hofn, where you may relax in the lonesome red chair art installation and explore the Hvalnes Lighthouse.

Day six of our Iceland itinerary is loaded with gorgeous drives and waterfalls. You'll begin by traveling along the East Fjords.

As you bike along, keep your eye on the seashore. That way, you'll be able to witness spectacular rock formations in the water, like the one near the Laekjavik Coast. And keep an eye out for the Kirkjubaer Church, one of the loveliest churches in Iceland.

As you reach the end of the East Fjords, you may climb to the Hengifoss and Litlanesfoss waterfalls. Both take a little of the trek (1.6 miles and 2.7 miles, respectively), but who doesn't want to see another spectacular Icelandic waterfall?

Finish off your day at Seydisfjordur, a town nestled in between two tall, snow-capped mountains. While there, you should travel to

the rainbow street to the gorgeous blue church. It is undoubtedly one of the nicest villages in Iceland!
lady in yellow skipping along the rainbow path to sky blue church Iceland itinerary

Dettifoss is a huge, strong waterfall found in North Iceland! There are two perspectives (East and West) where you may take in the power of Dettifoss. I suggest just picking one, considering the two parking lots are an hour apart. (That's simply how enormous the waterfall is!)

And if you think Dettifoss is stunning, you'll be even more blown away by Godafoss. Meaning "Waterfall of the Gods," this semi-circle of cascading water smashes into a soothing blue lake.

Stop three is the Myvatan Nature Baths. The Myvatan Nature Baths are essentially the North's counterpart of the Blue Lagoon. It's a terrific way to warm up after standing in the chilly air for much of the day.

Finally, join a whale-watching cruise in Husavik. Husavik is by far the greatest site to watch whales in Iceland. Keep an eye out for their spouts! You may spend the night at one of the numerous Akureyri Hotels, Iceland's second-largest city!
whale breaching

By day eight of our Iceland itinerary, you'll probably be a little bit worn out. You've seen waterfalls and glaciers and canyons! Oh my! So day eight provides you a little bit of time to take a rest.

The first destination on a relatively pleasant day is Alyderfoss. While Iceland has numerous waterfalls, Alyderfoss is a distinctive one. Flanked by unearthly basalt columns, this 65-foot waterfall flows into a stunning sky-blue pool.

After experiencing Alyderfoss, proceed to the city of Akureyri. Often named the capital of the North, there is so much to do in Akureyri. Visit the Akureyri Botanical Garden, the Akureyri Aviation Museum, the Akureyrarkirkja church, and the Christmas House.

While visiting the Snaefellness Peninsula, make sure to view the Kirkjufellsfoss Waterfall and Kirkjufell Mountain. If you have a little additional time, check out the street art in Hellissandur, the nature of Snaefellsjökull National Park, and the golden sand of Skardsvík Beach.

As you close up your vacation to Iceland, you'll go into the city of Reykjavik. The Sun Voyager sculpture, Hallgrimskirikja Church, and the HARPA Center should not be missed.

Venture out of the city again to rest in the Blue Lagoon, trek Glymur, or explore the Golden Circle.
walkway surrounded by lava rocks coated in snow

Itinerary for 2 Weeks in Iceland: RING ROAD and Westfjords

Day 1: Hot Springs And Waterfalls

Day 2: Start exploring the South Coast

Day 3: Keep Taking In The South Coast's Beauty

Day 4: Westman Islands Overnight

Day 5: Canyons And Skaftafell

Day 6: Southeast Iceland

Day 7: East Fjords

Day 8: Eastern Iceland

Day 9: Waterfalls And Whale Watching

Day 10: Westfjords

Day 11: Westfjords

Day 12: Snaefellsnes Peninsula

Day 13: Glymur

Day 14: Reykjavik And The Blue Lagoon

The first three days of this two-week Iceland schedule are similar to the first three days of the ten-day Iceland itinerary outlined above. As a matter of fact, the whole program is pretty similar to the ten days in Iceland itinerary. You'll simply have a bit more time to explore all of the beauty that Iceland has to offer.

Take a ferry to the Westman Islands, where you may gape at the stark black Heimaey Stave Church, explore Stórhöfði and watch for puffins, or even take a boat tour of the islands!

Experience the magnificence of the Fjadrargljufur and Mulagljufur Canyons. Then, drive to Skaftafell National Park, where you can enjoy a tour of an ice cave, get views of Icelandic wildlife, and climb glaciers and waterfalls.

While in Southeast Iceland on the sixth day of your two weeks in Iceland schedule, you may see the Jokulsarlon and Fjallsarlon Glacier Lagoons, Stokksnes mountain peaks, Diamond black sand beach, the Viking village film location, and the town of Hofn.

Drive along the East Fjords and keep your eye on the shore. Spot black sand beaches, crashing waves, and spectacular rock formations, such as the one along the

Laekjavik Coast. Then, come the excursions to the Hengifoss and Litlanesfoss waterfalls. End your day at Seydisfjordur, where you may traverse the rainbow street to the charming blue church.

Spend the morning continuing to explore the village of Seydisfjordur before traveling to the majestic Dettifoss waterfall. Then, travel to the Myvatan Nature Baths, the North's counterpart of the Blue Lagoon.

Start the ninth day with the Godafoss, the "Waterfall of the Gods." Then, embark on a boat and cruise out to observe some whales in Husavik. Finally, go over to the Geosea Spa. You may even be able to view some whales from afar while you warm up in the geothermal sea water-filled spas.

Why not end your day with a waterfall because you started it with one? Before spending the night in Akureyri, proceed to Alyderfoss.

The Westfjords is one of the most isolated places in Iceland. One of the greatest things to see in the Westfjords is viewing the Dynjandi waterfall. This large waterfall rushes down a series of natural obsidian stairs, making it unlike any other waterfall in Iceland.

From one type of water to another, go to the Drangsnes Hot Pots. This set of three natural hot pots is a fantastic way to warm up. And lastly, if you're expecting to view the charming, famous puffins, travel to the Latrabjarg Cliffs.

The under-the-radar Westfjords has so much to offer that you may spend two days in the region and not run out of things to do. First up on day two: Raudasandur Beach. While Iceland is renowned for its black sand beaches, Raudasandur Beach is a red sand beach!

Then, travel towards the capital city of the Westfjords, Ísafjörður. Ísafjörður is a charming seaside town packed with great cuisine, educational museums, and engaging music festivals.

As your two weeks in Iceland begin to come to a close, explore the Snaefellness Peninsula, which isn't too far outside of Reykjavik. Take a look at the Skardsvk Beach, Kirkjufellsfoss Waterfall, Kirkjufell Mountain, Hellissandur's street art, Snaefellsjökull National Park, and the street art there.

The four-hour-long journey to Glymur Waterfall and Canyon might be taxing, but it's worth the effort. Hike up hazardous cliffs, traverse broad rivers, and climb through caverns to reach the 650-foot Glymur Waterfall.

To find out your Iceland itinerary, head to the capital of Reykjavik. Be sure to view the

HARPA Center, Sun Voyager sculpture, and Hallgrimskirikja Church.

Then, if you still have some time left, rest in the Blue Lagoon or tour the Golden Circle.

No matter whatever Iceland itinerary you select, you're guaranteed to get your fill of nature and adventure throughout your stay in Iceland. We're happy that you've opted to visit our magnificent nation, regardless of the duration of your stay.

CPSIA information can be obtained
at www.ICGtesting.com
Printed in the USA
LVHW050850290123
738160LV00014B/595